100 ^{PLUS} PARTY GAMES

Fun & Easy Ideas for Parties & Holidays

Sally E. Stuart
and
Woody Young

Joy Publishing
San Juan Capistrano, California

Acknowledgements

The editors would like to thank
Kathy Dongarra and Craig White for their
assistance in compiling, editing and
illustrating this book.

Special

thanks to

Party Games Information Bureau

Library of Congress Cataloging-in-Publication Data

Stuart, Sally E.
    100 Plus Party Games.

    Bibliography: p.
    1. Games—United States. 2. Authors and
publishers—United States. I. Young, Woody C.,
CIP# 88-81502

ISBN 0-939513-60-9
ISBN 0-939513-61-7 (pbk.)

100 plus Party Games © 1988 Joy Publishing.
Illustrated drawings © 1984,1985,1986,1987,1988 California Clock Co.
Joy Publishing, 26131 Avenida Aeropuerto, Suite B,
San Juan Capistrano, California 92675.

TABLE OF CONTENTS

Smile with Kit-Cat®

A SMILE GIVES YOU THE PROPER INTRODUCTION!

© 1986 CALIFORNIA CLOCK CO.

Kit Cat™

To the Party Planner

The purpose of this book is to provide a wide variety of simple games and activities which can be easily adapted to any holiday, season, or party theme.

Included in the next few pages you will find a list of seasons and holidays with suggested symbols and colors to use in carrying out those themes.

The games included here are appropriate for a holiday party or get-together for various ages and group sizes. In addition, you will find a separate section for games to use in the classroom which will give a holiday emphasis to various learning activities.

Before selecting any games, please read the following section entitled, "How To Use This Book." The suggestions made there will help you adapt your chosen games more effectively.

How To Use This Book

★ ★ ★ ★ ★ ★ ★

★ ★ ★ ★ ★ ★ ★

Become familiar with these general instructions before selecting games from this book.

1. PICK YOUR HOLIDAY OR PARTY THEME. Every game in this book can be adapted to emphasize any holiday or season, as well as special party themes.

2. SELECT SUITABLE GAMES. A check of the table of contents will help you select the type of games most suitable to the situation and size of your group. Begin with a mixer to break the ice or help guests get acquainted. If your group is large, you may need to choose team games or relays. For a party, alternate active games (see Active Party Games) and quiet games (see Quiet Party Games or Word Games). Many of the quiet party games or word games are also appropriate for classroom use on special occasions.

3. CHOOSE SYMBOLS AND COLORS. After you have selected the game or games to fit your needs, look up the holiday you are celebrating in the next section of this book, entitled "Holidays and Seasons." Using the guidelines given there, select the symbols and colors you will need to carry out the game instructions. When instructed to cut holiday shapes from construction or other paper, always use appropriate holiday colors unless another color is specified.

4. CHANGE NAMES OF GAMES TO FIT HOLIDAY OR THEME. Because of the all-occasion nature of these games, most titles use the all-inclusive word "holiday". When introducing the game to your group, replace the word "holiday" with the name of the particular holiday you are celebrating; i.e., Holiday Symphony would become Christmas Symphony, etc. Likewise, when "holiday symbol" is used, it should be replaced with the appropriate symbol, such as Holiday Symbol Drop to Pumpkin Drop or Turkey Drop.

5. USE APPROPRIATE TEAM NAMES. To give a holiday emphasis to team games you may wish to use, but which are not readily adapted to a theme, give each team a holiday-related name, like "The Stars" and "The Bells," or a holiday color name, such as "The Red Team" and "The Green Team."

6. PATTERNS FOR PARTY DECORATIONS. Toward the back of this book is a section of easy to use symbol patterns. They can be traced to make patterns for name tags or game pieces. Follow these easy directions to enlarge or reduce a pattern as needed:

Trace the pattern you want on a sheet of typing or tracing paper and then use the grid pattern (page 83) to make a 1'' grid over the design.

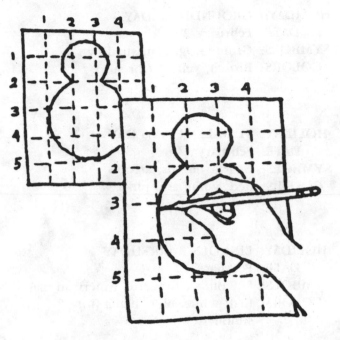

Square off a piece of paper the size you wish the pattern to be. If you want the pattern larger, make the squares larger. If you want the pattern smaller, make the squares smaller. For example, if you want your pattern twice as large, use two-inch squares, or three times as large, use 3-inch squares. If you want it only half as big, use ½ inch squares. Place your squared-off sheet next to the grid-covered pattern you have traced and reproduce the design on your sheet, one square at a time.

7. TIPS FOR ORGANIZATIONS. Schools or churches may find it helpful to make up some of the game props ahead of time to have available for teachers and classes. Provide a storage place for reusable items from parties, boxed or filed by holiday name. A pattern file of enlarged holiday shapes would also be helpful.

Holiday and Seasons

HOLIDAY:: GROUNDHOG DAY
    DATE: February 2
SYMBOLS: Groundhog, sun, shadow
  COLORS: Brown, yellow (for sun)

HOLIDAY: ST. VALENTINE'S DAY
    DATE: February 14
SYMBOLS: Hearts, cupids, arrows
  COLORS: Red, white and pink

HOLIDAY: LINCOLN'S BIRTHDAY
    DATE: February 12
SYMBOLS: Lincoln's silhouette, American flag
  COLORS: Red, white, blue, black (for silhouette)

☆ ☆ ☆ ☆ ☆ ☆ ☆ ☆ ☆

HOLIDAY: PRESIDENT'S DAY
    DATE: Third Monday of February
SYMBOLS: See Lincoln's Birthday and Washington's Birthday
  COLORS: See Lincoln's Birthday and Washington's Birthday

☆ ☆ ☆ ☆ ☆ ☆ ☆ ☆ ☆

HOLIDAY: WASHINGTON'S BIRTHDAY
    DATE: February 22
SYMBOLS: Washington's silhouette, cherry tree, hatchet, American flag
  COLORS: Red, white, blue, black (for silhouette)

HOLIDAY: ST. PATRICK'S DAY
 DATE: March 17
SYMBOLS: Shamrocks, leprechauns, green top
         hats
 COLORS: Green

SPRING FUN

HOLIDAY: BEGINNING OF SPRING
 DATE: March 20
SYMBOLS: Flowers, baby animals
 COLORS: Pastels, especially pink, yellow,
         lavender, light blue, light green

HOLIDAY: EASTER
 DATE: Between March 22 and April 25 (Set
        on the first Sunday after the first full
        moon on or after March 21.)
SYMBOLS: Resurrection-cross, lilies, Easter
         baskets, bunnies, eggs, flowers, baby
         animals
 COLORS: Pastels, purple

HOLIDAY: MAY DAY
    DATE: May 1
SYMBOLS: Baskets of flowers
  COLORS: Any bright colors or pastels

HOLIDAY: MOTHER'S DAY
    DATE: Second Sunday of May
SYMBOLS: Mother's silhouette, flowers
          (especially carnations)
  COLORS: Any bright colors or pastels

HOLIDAY: MEMORIAL DAY
    DATE: Last Monday in May
SYMBOLS: White crosses, flowers, flags
  COLORS: Red, white, blue

HOLIDAY: FLAG DAY
    DATE: June 14
SYMBOLS: American flag
  COLORS: Red, white, blue

HOLIDAY: FATHER'S DAY
    DATE: Third Sunday in June
SYMBOLS: Fathers with children
  COLORS: Any color

HOLIDAY: BEGINNING OF SUMMER
  DATE: June 21
SYMBOLS: Sun, flowers
  COLORS: Bright colors, white

HOLIDAY: INDEPENDENCE DAY
  DATE: July 4
SYMBOLS: Firecrackers, skyrockets, flags, bunting
  COLORS: Red, white, blue

And the rock– ets' red glare,

HOLIDAY: LABOR DAY
  DATE: First Monday of September
SYMBOLS: Men in work clothes, tools
COLORS: Any color

AUTUMN
FUN

HOLIDAY: BEGINNING OF AUTUMN
  DATE: September 22
SYMBOLS: Fall leaves, rakes, bushel baskets
COLORS: Gold, brown, orange

HOLIDAY: COLUMBUS DAY
DATE: October 12
SYMBOLS: Three ships
COLORS: Any color

HOLIDAY: HALLOWEEN
DATE: October 31
SYMBOLS: Jack-o-lanterns, witches, ghosts, skeletons, owls, black cats, corn shocks
COLORS: Black, orange

HOLIDAY: VETERAN'S DAY
DATE: November 11
SYMBOLS: Men in uniform, flags, bunting
COLORS: Red, white, blue

HOLIDAY: THANKSGIVING
   DATE: Fourth Thursday of November
         (Canada-Second Monday of October)
SYMBOLS: Turkey, pilgrims, Indians, pumpkins,
         corn shocks, cornucopia
 COLORS: Brown, orange, gold

WINTER
FUN

HOLIDAY: BEGINNING OF WINTER
   DATE: December 21
SYMBOLS: Snowflakes, snowmen, hats and
         gloves
 COLORS: Blue, white

HOLIDAY: CHRISTMAS
   DATE: December 25
SYMBOLS: Birth of Jesus Christ—Star, creche,
         Wise-men, shepherds. baby, angels,
         Santa Claus, tree ornaments, bells,
         holly, presents, reindeer/sleigh
 COLORS: Red, green

HOLIDAY: NEW YEAR'S EVE
   DATE: December 31
SYMBOLS: Baby New Year, Old Man Time,
         hourglass, party hats and horns
 COLORS: Any bright colors (especially - Gold
         & Silver)

All-Occasion Party Plans

Invitations

Blow up balloons in the proper holiday color(s), and hold tightly shut. Using a felt-tip ten, draw a simple holiday shape on one side of the balloon, and the invitation on the other side. Deflate the balloons and mail one to each guest in an envelope. If desired, decorate envelopes with holiday seals.

Decorations

1. Cut holiday shapes from construction paper or felt and pin them to the tablecloth on your refreshment table.
2. Hang mobiles of holiday shapes around the room.
3. Hang streamers in holiday colors.
4. Use holiday shapes for name tags, place mats, etc.
5. Attach self-adhesive holiday seals to plain white or holiday-colored paper plates, cups, and napkins.

Refreshments

1. Have guests decorate cupcakes in the holiday motif.

2. Frost and decorate large, plain cookies.

3. Make large cutout cookies using a holiday-shaped cookie cutter. Before baking, have guests decorate them with egg-yolk paint. (Beat egg yolks with one teaspoon of water per yolk. Divide into individual dishes and color each with food coloring in a variety of appropriate colors.) Guests "paint" their cookies using clean paintbrushes. Bake and serve later for refreshments.

4. Paint a bare tree branch white, gold, or black and stand it in a bucket of sand. Make popcorn balls and wrap individually in clear plastic wrap or cellophane. Add one or more self-adhesive holiday seals to each wrapped ball and hang from the tree limbs, using yarn in holiday colors. The bucket of sand may be covered with holiday wrap.

Smile with Kit-Cat®

A SMILE IS THE SHORTEST DISTANCE BETWEEN TWO PEOPLE.

© 1986 CALIFORNIA CLOCK CO.

Kit-Cat™

MIXERS

⭐⭐⭐⭐⭐⭐⭐⭐⭐⭐⭐⭐⭐

★ ★ ★ ★ ★ ★ ★ ★ ★ ★ ★

Broken Holiday Symbols

Cut out a quantity of construction paper symbols (such as hearts, pumpkins, trees, etc.) to fit the holiday, half as many as expected guests. Give each person half a symbol. At the signal, each one must find the person with the matching half of his shape. When they get together, each of the partners must tell the other his name and two things about himself. They each write the information learned on their half of the shape, tape the halves together, and then display them on the wall or bulletin board.

Find the Holiday Symbols

Cut out five small holiday symbols (small enough to be concealed in the palm of the hand), and give them secretly to five guests as they arrive. When everyone is present, tell them that five people in the group are holding a symbol, and will give it to the tenth person who shakes their hand during the next few minutes. At the end of the allotted time, symbols may be redeemed for a small prize.

Note: If most of the members of your group are strangers, require that they exchange names every time they shake hands. The number of hidden symbols and the number of handshakes required to obtain a symbol may be increased or decreased according to the size of your group.

Holiday Feet

Divide the group into pairs and give each couple a water-color felt-tip pen in an appropriate holiday color. Tell couples to decide which of them will be the "artist" and which will be the "canvas". After they have decided, explain that the "canvas" must remove one shoe and sock so the "artist" may draw a holiday design on the sole of his foot. Give a prize for the best design. To add to the fun, also give prizes for the biggest foot, smallest foot, cleanest foot, or whatever fits. The prize ribbons can be hung from the big toes by attached string loops.

Holiday Detectives

Blow up half as many holiday-colored balloons as you expect guests. Draw a holiday shape on each balloon using a felt-tip marker and write the name of a guest inside the shape. (You will be using the names of only half the guests. Keep a list of which ones.) Deflate the balloons and hide them around the room. When the guests arrive, have those whose names are on the balloons sit in the middle of the floor, not too closely together. Explain to the others that they must find a balloon, inflate it to read the name (it must be inflated), find that person, and sit down next to him on the floor. The last one to sit down is the loser and may be given a small magnifying glass as a booby prize.

● ● ● ● ● ● ● ● ● ● ● ● ● ● ● ● ● ● ●

● ● ● ● ● ● ● ● ● ● ● ● ● ● ● ● ● ●

Pretty Baby

Cut enough holiday shapes to have one for each guest. Ask everyone to bring a baby picture of himself. Collect the pictures as guests arrive (before anyone sees them), and attach each one to a holiday shape using picture corners or double-sided tape. Distribute the shape/pictures among the guests, and tell them they must find the person in their picture. Give a prize to the first one to identify his "mystery" friend, if you like. When everyone has found his person, have him write the person's name and two other things about him on the shape around the outside of the picture. When finished, the shapes can be pinned on their owners as name tags. The pictures will serve as good icebreakers during the rest of the party.

Autograph Symbols

Give each guest a holiday shape cut from a 9 x 12 inch sheet of construction paper, and a pencil or crayon. At the signal, each one is to try to get as many different autographs on his shape as possible within a set time limit. The time limit will vary depending on the size of your group, but keep it short enough that they will have trouble getting around to everyone. The one who gets the most names is the winner. You may also recognize those with the most boys or girls names.

○ ○ ○ ○ ○ ○ ○ ○

★ ★ ★ ★ ★ ★ ★ ★ ★ ★ ★

Who Am I?

Make each guest a large, construction paper name tag in a holiday shape. Write his name in bold letters across the middle of the shape and pin the tag to his back. Give each guest a nylon-tip pen or crayon. At the signal, everyone is to start writing something about himself on other people's name tags. Tell them to keep it brief, such as: brown house, red bicycle, Colton School, three sisters, etc. At the end of a set time limit, each person removes his name tag, and signs it. The first one to identify the writer of each phrase, and get his signature, is the winner. In front of the group, let him introduce each of those people and tell what each wrote on his tag.

Holiday Crossword

Give each guest a holiday shape cut from a 9 x 12 inch sheet of construction paper. Print the name of the holiday, vertically, down the center of each shape. At the signal, everyone looks for someone in the group whose name begins with one of the holiday letters on his shape, and writes it in the proper place. If they are unable to find anyone whose name starts with a given letter, they may substitute someone who has that letter somewhere within his name. The first one to fill in every letter of the holiday is the winner.

★ ★ ★ ★

★ ★ ★ ★

Holiday Name Tag Jumble

Decorate an open box appropriately for the holiday and cut out holiday-shaped name tags from construction paper. Have each guest put his name on a tag and drop it into the box. Mix up the tags. Each person pulls out a tag (not his own) and goes looking for the correct person to pin it on.

A Good Word

Write each guest's name on a slip of paper and drop it into a hat or other container. Everyone draws out a name, being careful not to get his own. Give each guest a sheet of typing paper with the name of the holiday written vertically in large letters along the left-hand side of the sheet. Instruct the guests to write a list of adjectives describing the person whose name they drew, using the holiday letters on the sheet as the first letter of each adjective. When the lists are completed, each one should introduce his person by telling his name and reading his list of descriptive words.

21

Holiday Musical

As guests arrive, hand each a slip of paper on which you have written the name of a well-known holiday or seasonal song. Use several songs, but give the name of the same song to three or more people, depending on the size of your group. The object is for each guest to find the others in his group (those who were assigned the same song). When all the groups have formed, give them a few minutes to get acquainted and to plan their "performance". Then give each group the opportunity to sing their song for the other guests. You may give a prize or special recognition for the best act.

Holiday Match

Collect a variety of holiday-related objects or pictures, being sure you have an identical mate for each item collected. Distribute the individual objects among the guests, and instruct them to find the person who has the object identical to their own. That person will become their partner for the next game.

Where Are You?

Make up a list of appropriate holiday songs, or songs that match your theme. Write the name of each song on two separate slips of paper. If you want boy/girl couples, pass out one set to the boys and the other set to the girls. If it doesn't matter, distribute at random. When each guest has a slip, he is to sing, hum or whistle his assigned tune, and at the same time try to find the person who is performing the same tune.

Famous Names

As each guest enters the room, pin the name of a famous person on his or her back. The rules are that the participant can ask each person in the room one question that can be answered by either a "yes" or "no". (Example: "Is this famous person still alive?"). After the participant receives his answer, he must move on and ask another person the next question. The first participant to guess his "identity" gets a prize.

Person to Person Scavenger Hunt

Give each person a copy of this Scavenger Hunt handout. Instruct them to walk around the room and try to find someone in the group who matches each question (or as many as possible).

Offering a prize for the person finding the most similarities is always fun.

○ ○ ○ ○ ○ ○ ○

Scavenger Hunt Handout

1. Someone with the same color eyes. _____
2. Someone born in the same state. _____
3. Someone who has the same astrological sign. _____
4. Someone who likes the same sport. _____
5. Someone who has the same favorite dessert. _____
6. Someone who has the same number of letters in his name. _____
7. Someone who is the same height. _____
8. Someone who is the youngest in his family. _____

9. Someone who would like to write a book. _____
10. Someone who has seen the same movie at least three times. _____
11. Someone who has traveled outside the United States. _____
12. Someone who likes to ski. _____
13. Someone who is an only child. _____
14. Someone who can speak two languages. _____
15. Someone who likes to cook. _____

● ● ● ● ● ●

Smile with Kit-Cat®

WHEN YOU MEET SOMEONE WITHOUT A SMILE GIVE THEM ONE OF YOURS!

© 1986 CALIFORNIA CLOCK CO.

RELAYS

2

★ ★ ★ ★ ★

Holiday Chopstick Relay

Cut a holiday shape from construction paper for each team. Divide the group into two or more equal teams. Line up teams at one end of the play area, and mark a goal line at the other end. Give the first person on each team the holiday shape and a pair of chopsticks or two unsharpened pencils. At the signal, they must hold the shape between the two sticks (using only one hand), and run to the goal line and back. Each player makes the same run. Anyone dropping the shape in the course of his run must stop, go back to his team and begin again. The first team to finish is the winner.

Variation: To make it more difficult for older guests, have a leader stand with his back to the group frequently calling out new instructions that must be followed, such as walk, crawl, hop on one foot, skip, walk backwards, etc.

Holiday Balloon Walk

Inflate a number of balloons in holiday colors and draw a holiday design on each one with a felt-tip pen. Divide the group into two or more equal teams. At the signal, each person must carry the balloon between his knees to the goal line and back. If the balloon breaks, he must come back for a new one and start over. The first team to finish is the winner. A large balloon for each team member would be an appropriate prize.

Variations: (A) Play as an individual competition, using a stopwatch to time each competitor. The one with the shortest time is the winner. (B) Set up an obstacle course for players to walk through on their way to the goal line.

Holiday Race Track

Cut two or more holiday shapes from typing paper, and write a holiday-related team name on each shape, such as the "Owls", the "Pumpkins" or the "Ghosts". Divide the group into two or more equal teams, and line them up at one end of the room. Lay a shape on the floor in front of each team and give the first person in each line an inexpensive paper plate. (Draw or paste holiday designs on the plates to correspond with the team names.) The object is to use the plate as a fan to blow the shape to the goal line and back. The plate is handed to the next person in line, and play continues until the first team finished is declared the winner.

Holiday Straw Relay

Cut two or more four-inch holiday shapes from construction paper. Divide the group into two or more equal teams. Give each player a drinking straw, and each team one of the paper shapes. One at a time the team members pick up the shape by sucking through the straw, then carry it to the goal line and back. If they drop it, they must start over. The first team to have all players complete the task successfully is the winner.

▲▲▲▲▲▲▲▲▲

Holiday Verse Relay

Cut out six holiday shapes from construction paper. Write a holiday verse or saying on each shape, keeping them all about the same length. Put three of the shapes into each of the two envelopes or flat paper bags. Divide the group into two equal teams, and give the first person in each line one of the envelopes. At the signal, that person removes the shapes from the envelope and reads all three verses aloud. He then returns them to the envelope and hands them to the next person in line who must repeat the reading. The first team to finish reading is the winner. The noise and confusion of two players reading something different out loud just adds to the merriment.

Holiday Beanbag Relay

Make two or more holiday-shaped, felt beanbags. Divide the group into two or more equal teams and have each team line up in separate lines with the players one behind the other. Give a beanbag to the first person in each line. The object is to pass the beanbag down the line from the first person to the last, and back again. Before each round, the leader calls out the way in which the bag is to be passed: over the head, between the legs, down the right or left. If anyone passes it incorrectly during that round, the beanbag goes back to the front of the line and that team starts over. The first team to get its beanbag back to the first person in line is the winner.

Spear the Holiday Sweets

Put holiday-colored jelly beans into two bowls that have been decorated with self-adhesive holiday seals. Divide the group into two equal relay teams, and give each team one bowl. Teams line up, and each person is given a round, wooden toothpick. At the signal, the first person in each line spears a jelly bean with the toothpick and feeds it to the person next to him. He then passes the bowl to the second player who feeds one to the next person, and so on. The team to reach the end of its line first is the winner.

Holiday Pops

Give each guest a lunch-size paper bag and set out some crayons or felt-tip pens. Have them decorate their bags appropriately for the holiday. When bags are completed, divide the group into relay teams. The object of the game is for each person at the front of the line to blow up his bag as he runs toward the end of his line. When he reaches the end of the line he is to pop it. If the sack doesn't pop the first time, he must keep trying until he is successful. The next person in each line repeats the action as soon as he hears the previous bag pop. Play continues until player number one is back at the front of the line.

Holiday Balloon/Broom Relay

Inflate a number of balloons in holiday colors and draw on holiday designs with a black felt-tip pen. Decorate appropriately for the holiday one broom for each team. Divide the group into two or more relay teams and give each team a broom and one balloon. At the signal, the first player on each team must use the broom to sweep the balloon across the goal line at the other end of the room, and then use the stick end to keep the balloon off the floor as he returns it to the next player. (If a balloon pops in transport, the player must return to where he started, get a new balloon, and begin again.) First team to have all players finish is the winner.

Holiday Basket

Divide the group into two or more relay teams and give the first person in each line a basket of holiday items, or shapes cut from construction paper. At the signal, that person takes one shape from the basket and passes it to the next person. He immediately reaches for a second one which follows closely behind the first, and so on. The shapes are passed from person to person, down the line, one after the other, until the last person in each line is holding all the shapes from that team's basket. (No person is allowed to hold or pass more than one shape at a time except for this anchor person.) As soon as he has received the final shape, he starts passing them back in the same way. First team to return all shapes to their basket is the winner.

Smile with Kit-Cat®

A SMILE IS AN EASY THING TO GET BEHIND!

© 1986 CALIFORNIA CLOCK CO.

Kit-Cat™

TEAM GAMES

Holiday Jigsaw Puzzles

Find or draw two large holiday pictures or figures and cut them into an equal number of irregular-shaped pieces to make puzzles. Put each puzzle into a separate manila envelope, divide the group into two teams, and give an envelope to each team. At the signal, each team works to put its puzzle together. First team finished is the winner. Trade puzzles and repeat.

☆ ☆ ☆

Holiday Trail of Clues

Divide the group into two or more teams and give each team captain a clue written on a holiday-shaped piece of construction paper. That clue will instruct the team where to go to pick up the next holiday-shaped clue, etc. Provide at least ten clues (a different set for each team) leading to a "treasure" at the end. The "treasure" could be a special holiday treat, instructions for the next game, refreshments, or whatever fits into your plans.

Holiday Grab-It (or Grab Bag)

Cut a six to ten inch holiday shape from poster board or heavy cardboard. Divide the group into two equal teams and line them up facing each other across the room. Number off the players in each line, being sure each one knows his number. Lay the holiday shape in the middle of the floor between the two teams. When the leader calls a number, the player on each team who was given that number runs to the center, tries to grab the shape, and runs back to his own line before the other player tags him. He may only be tagged while the object is in his hand. If he returns to his line without being tagged, he wins a point for his team. If he is tagged, the point goes to the other team. The leader should continue to call out numbers until every player has had at least one turn. Team earning the most points is the winner.

Variation: To play Grab Bag, decorate a lunch bag, fill it with wrapped, holiday candies, and staple the top closed. Use the bag in the game above in place of the holiday shape. The winning team gets to share the candy in the bag.

32

Holiday Gift Packages

Write a special message (perhaps the location of a prize) on two slips of paper and enclose each in a small box. Gift wrap the boxes in holiday wrap and put each into a slightly larger box. Wrap and tie those boxes and continue wrapping with an equal number of boxes, wrappings and ties. (Larger boxes may be wrapped in newspaper and decorated with appropriate holiday designs in crayon or water-color marker.)

Divide the group into two teams and give the large wrapped package to the first person on each team. At the signal they begin unwrapping the packages. After a short time, give a signal for that person to pass the package to the next person in line, who continues the unwrapping. (Do not allow them to unwrap more than one box at a time.) Continue signaling the time to change so everyone will have a chance to unwrap. First team to reach the message is the winner. **Note:** *If you use strong ribbon or yarn, and tie it securely, it will make the unwrapping more difficult.*

★ ★ ★ ★ ★

Holiday Scavenger Hunt

Divide the group into two or more teams of five to ten people. Give each team a list of items to find. Make all items relate in some way to the holiday, or of a holiday color. If it is a seasonal party, use nature items associated with that season. Teams go door-to-door, or around the room or play area to find their listed items. Set a time limit so all will be back within a reasonable length of time. The first team to return with all its items, or the most items, within the time limit is the winner.

Fill the Holiday Sack

Hang up or set out on a table in the middle of the room, two large cloth or paper bags decorated appropriately for the holiday. The bags should be decorated so each is a contrasting color, i.e., red and green, black and orange, red and white, etc. Before the guests arrive, hide a quantity of wrapped holiday candy all around the room. (If you cannot get candy in the team colors, you must add a piece of yarn or paper in the proper colors.) Hide an equal number of pieces in each color.

Divide the group into two teams and designate the team colors by pinning ribbons or small holiday shapes on each guest in the proper colors. Start playing an appropriate holiday song on a tape or record player, and then start everyone marching around the room. Every time you stop the music, the players should stop marching around the room and run to find the hidden candy. Every time they find a piece they must put it in the team bag before going back for another. They are not allowed to pick up any candy of the opposing team's color. When the music resumes, they must immediately come back to the circle and start marching. Continue stopping and starting the music until all, or most of the candy has been found. At the end, the team with the most pieces in its bag is the winner. Each team may then divide its candy between all of its team members.

★ ★ ★ ★ ★ ★ ★ ★ ★ ★ ★ ★ ★ ★

Find the Holiday Shapes

Cut out an equal number of two different holiday shapes (or the same shape in two different colors). Divide the group into two teams and assign each a shape (or color). Pin one of the appropriate shapes to each team member. At the signal, each team is instructed to find all the shapes assigned to them, which were previously hidden around the room. Tell them how many there are. First team to find all their shapes is the winner. If neither team has located all its shapes within a reasonable length of time, set a time limit and the one finding the most within that limit is the winner. You may want to star one shape for each team and give the finder of that particular shape a special prize.

Decorate It

Divide the group into teams of about five players each. Give each team a paper bag of appropriate materials and decorations to fit the holiday. Include scissors, tape and a selection of newspapers, holiday-colored crepe paper, toilet paper, and trims and items suitable to the holiday.

Each group chooses one person to be "decorated" as a Christmas tree, Thanksgiving turkey, valentine, jack-o-lantern, etc. At the signal, each team decorates its chosen person. Give them three or four minutes to complete their masterpiece, and then have the group or an outside judge pick the winner. Be sure to take pictures!

Holiday Art

Divide the group into two or more teams and provide each group with a large pad of paper and crayons or felt-tip markers. At the signal, each group sends an "artist" to the leader who whispers to each one the name of a holiday-related object to draw. The "artists" run back to their team and start drawing the object as fast as they can. They are not allowed to say anything or to write anything on the paper except for their picture. As soon as the group recognizes the object, they yell it out. The first group to yell wins that round, and the same or another artist is sent back to the leader for a new assignment. Play as long as interest is running high, and keep score of the winning teams. Prizes for the winning team could be holiday-related, or possibly boxes of crayons or water paints.

Smile with Kit-Cat®

A SMILE CAN'T BE COPIED, ONLY ORIGINALS COUNT!

© 1986 CALIFORNIA CLOCK CO.

Kit-Cat™

QUIET PARTY GAMES

★★★★★★★★★★★★★

Holiday Egg Show

Eggs need not be limited to Easter celebrations. Provide each guest with at least one hard-boiled egg, and set out a quantity of permanent felt-tip pens. Have them use the pens to decorate the eggs appropriately for the holiday. Make a stand for each egg by stapling together the ends of a 1 x 5 inch strip of construction paper. Display all the finished eggs on stands on a table or other suitable area. Let guests vote on the best ones, or have a special "judge" pick the winners and award ribbons.

Holiday Shape Drop

Cut ten small holiday shapes from construction paper, and hold each one in a clip-type clothespin. Decorate a quart jar, or other suitable container, in the holiday motif. Have guests take turns standing over the jar and dropping the clothespins/shapes from waist height. Each pin that goes into the jar is worth ten points. The guest earning the most points is the winner. If there is a tie, let them play off until one is declared the winner. **Note:** *For a large group, you may want to prepare more than one jar and set of clothespins.*

It's In the Box

Decorate a number of shoe boxes appropriately for the holiday, and place a different object inside each one. (Boxes should be taped shut or wrapped before decorating.) Seat guests in a circle, and start passing one box around. They may shake it if they wish, and guess what's in it any time they have an idea. The leader should give a hint periodically, and tell when their guesses are "hot" or "cold". The first one to guess correctly wins that round, and another box is started around.

Holiday Luck

Cut several holiday shapes from construction paper. On one side of each shape write either a stunt to perform or a reward. Turn shapes upside-down and spread out on a table, or in the middle of the floor, or place in a holiday-decorated box or basket. Each guest, in turn, selects a shape and receives the reward, or performs the stunt as instructed.

String Chewing Contest

Inflate a balloon for each guest and draw holiday shapes on it with a felt-tip pen. Tie a two-foot long piece of lightweight string to each balloon. Each player is given a balloon and instructed to hold the end of the string in his teeth with the balloon hanging down in front of him. At the signal, he must "eat" the string in order to bring the balloon up to his mouth. No hands allowed. First one to do so is the winner.

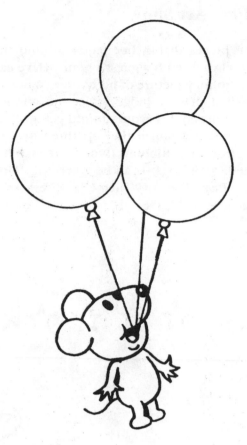

Holiday Sound Effects

Have the group form a circle and choose one person to be "it". Have him stand in the center of the circle with a holiday paper napkin. "It" opens the napkin, throws it high into the air, and starts making the appropriate holiday sound effect (i.e., Turkey—gobble; July 4th—Bang! Bang!; etc.), or starts singing a holiday song. Players are to imitate the holiday sound as long as the napkin is in the air; but when it touches the floor they must stop immediately. The first player still making a sound after the napkin lands becomes "it". Repeat until most players have been "caught".

Are You Alert?

This is a fun and quick exercise to stress the importance of being alert and observant. Before the meeting, prepare a tray of 20 unrelated items and cover the tray.

Tell participants that they will have one minute to look at the objects on a tray. They will then be asked to write down as many things as they can remember. Explain that there will be a prize for the person who remembers the most items.

Uncover the tray and give the group exactly one minute before covering it again. Instruct them to write down as many items as they can remember. Ask for volunteers to read their lists.

☆ ☆ ☆ ☆

Holiday Art Show

Tape pieces of butcher paper around the room, and label each with a guest's name. Have each guest draw a holiday picture of his choice. When everyone is finished, have a judge select the winners. With young children, everyone should get a ribbon. With older ones, recognize the top three places, or the number desired. Ribbons (which are attached to the finished "paintings") can be given for "Most Original", "Best Use of Theme", "Best of Show", "Judge's Award", etc.

On a Dark Holiday Night

Give a sheet of typing paper and pencil to each guest. (Guests should be seated at a table or have a magazine or other sturdy surface to write on.) When everyone is ready, turn out the lights. It should be too dark to see well. The leader then calls out the name of a holiday object for the guests to draw on the papers. After enough time has elapsed, he calls out additional items, one at a time until the picture is complete. Turn on the lights, let guests look at their own pictures, and then share them with each other. A prize may be given for the least recognizable.

Holiday Symphony

Choose a conductor to lead the group in a holiday or seasonal song. At his signal everyone stops singing except the one person he points to. That person must continue to sing, hum, or whistle the tune. If he doesn't, he trades places with the conductor.

★ ★ ★ ★

Holiday Greetings

Seat guests in a circle and choose one to be "it". "It" stands in front of any person and gives the appropriate holiday greeting: "Happy Valentine's Day to you"; "Merry Christmas and Happy New Year"; "Happy Easter to you"; etc. The person being addressed must respond: "And the same to you," before "it" has finished his greeting. If he doesn't, the two must trade places. If he does, "it" must go on to someone else and repeat his greeting.

How Many?

Fill a clear glass jar with holiday candies, and decorate the jar with self-adhesive holiday seals. (Be careful not to put on so many seals that you hide the contents of the jar.) Set the jar on a table with some slips of paper and a few pencils. Sometime during the party, give each guest an opportunity to write on a slip of paper his name and his estimate of the number of candies. The one who comes closest to the actual number wins the jar of candy.

Holiday Lollipops

Purchase holiday lollipops or plain cellophane-wrapped lollipops and add a holiday seal to each wrapper. Have enough for at least one per guest. Using felt-tip markers, put red dots on the ends of half the lollipop sticks, put a green dot on the end of one stick, and leave the rest plain. Poke all the sticks into a Styrofoam cone or slab, or into a decorated, cardboard box deep enough to permit the lollipops to stand upright with the ends of the sticks hidden. You will need enough small prizes for the plain sticks, better prizes for the red-tipped sticks, and a grand prize for the green-tipped stick. Each guest draws out a lollipop and is awarded a prize according to the color on the end of his stick.

☆ ☆ ☆ ☆ ☆

Holiday Masks

Give each guest a plain white paper plate, two 12-inch pieces of string, and some crayons or felt-tipped markers. Have each guest make a holiday mask. If scissors are available, they may cut out the eyes and other facial features. If not, features can be drawn on. When completed, string can be tied to each side, and the masks worn for the judging. Give a prize for the mask that best displays the holiday theme.

A Holiday Minute

Give each guest a sheet of typing paper, and a crayon in the appropriate holiday color. At the signal, everyone is to outline as many as possible of the assigned holiday shape on his paper for exactly one minute. When time has been called, everyone counts the number of shapes he has drawn. The one with the most shapes is the winner.

Holiday Headdresses

Give each guest a medium-sized, brown paper grocery bag, and have him roll down the top edge to make a hat. Provide a variety of items for decorating, and have each one decorate his hat appropriately for the holiday. Give a prize for the most original creation. **Note:** *As a variation, tell each guest to come to the party in a decorated hat, and give a prize for the most outlandish.*

Torn Holiday Shapes

Have everyone select a partner, and give each couple a sheet of holiday-colored construction paper. At the signal, they are to work together to tear out an assigned holiday shape from the paper. The catch is that they may each use only one hand. (The other is to be held behind their back.) One must use his right hand, while the other uses his left. Award prizes for the biggest shape, smallest shape, best looking, most unusual, etc.

43

Holiday Gift Wrap

Give each couple some newspaper, holiday-colored ribbon or yarn, and an unusual shaped, hard-to-wrap object. When possible, use holiday-related items, such as a pumpkin or large heart-shaped box. Otherwise, pick anything that would be difficult to wrap: a broom, wastebasket, hammer, large boot, shovel, large frying pan, etc. Try to keep the degree of difficulty about even. If you wish, assign each item a number and have guests draw for their item. At the signal, couples race to see who can completely wrap and tie their gift first. No part of the item may be exposed. After the winning couple has been named, have everyone go on and finish wrapping their gift. They will then continue and decorate their wrapped gift appropriately for the holiday. The unusual shape of the gifts should suggest some unique decorations. Give another prize for the most creative decorating job.

Holiday Fashion Show

Divide the group into couples. Give each couple a stack of newspapers, a handful of toothpicks, and a pair of scissors. Allow ten minutes for one person to dress the other in a holiday costume, using only the supplies provided. When the time is up, have a fashion parade, and let the guests select the best costume.

Holiday Bag Art

Gather enough grocery-size paper bags for each guest. (Bags must be blank on at least one large side.) Give each guest a bag and an appropriate, holiday-colored crayon. Instruct them to open the bag and put it over their head with the blank side in front of their face. When they have the bag in place, they are to use the crayon to draw a holiday design (heart, tree, shamrock, bunny, etc.) on the side of the bag over their face. When completed, collect the bags from the artists without letting them see the results. Write each one's name on the back of their bag, and display them with the names hidden. See how many can recognize their own work. Award prizes if you like.

★★★★★★★★★★★★★★

★★★★★★★★★★★★

Holiday Soap Carving

Give each guest a bar of soap and a paring knife. Have them carve a holiday shape from the soap. Give a prize for the best one.

I Want My Body

Give each person a 9 x 12 inch sheet of white construction paper, and ask him to fold it in half the short way, and then in half again so the sheet is divided in fourths (folded sheet will be 9 x 3 inches).

The object is to draw a person dressed in an appropriate holiday costume, but each guest will draw only one-fourth of the finished picture. Seat guests around a table or in a circle on the floor with a magazine to write on. Have them unfold their sheet of paper and draw a holiday hat on the top fourth, being sure that enough of the hat goes over the fold-line so the next person will know where to draw. (Each section will need to overlap the fold for the same reason.) When the hat is completed, that section is turned under on the fold line, and the paper is passed to the person on the right who proceeds to draw the face. The third person draws the body, and the fourth person draws the legs and feet and labels it with a name at the bottom. When the pictures are completed, pass them around the circle for everyone to see. Have the group select the most original holiday character.

Holiday ABC's

Make up a set of alphabet cards on four to six inch holiday shapes cut from poster board or heavy construction paper. Eliminate the hard letters like Q, X, V, and Z. Have the group sit in a circle with one person standing in the center holding the stack of mixed-up alphabet shapes. He shows the top card to one player in the circle who must immediately respond with a holiday-related word that begins with that letter. If he does so, the center person goes to another player and displays the next card on the pile. When a player can't answer, or answers too slowly, he must trade places with the center person.

Holiday Pin-up

Adapt the familiar game of "Pin the Tail on the Donkey" to fit your holiday or seasonal celebration. Use these ideas to spark your imagination for figures to replace the traditional donkey and tail: Valentines—arrow in cupid's hand; St. Patrick's Day—hat on a leprechaun; Spring—bee in the center of a flower; Easter—tail on a bunny; May Day—basket on a doorknob; July 4th—Liberty Bell at Philadelphia on a U.S. map; Halloween— nose on a jack-o-lantern; Thanksgiving—tail feathers on a turkey; Christmas—star on a tree top.

To play, draw the appropriate figure on a large sheet of poster board, minus the part to be added, and hang on the wall or a bulletin board. One at a time the players are blindfolded and given the part to be added. After being spun around three times, he is faced toward the figure. The object is to pin the piece in his hand as close to the proper place on the figure as possible. Write each guest's name by the pinhole when the piece is removed and passed on to the next guest. The player coming closest to the exact spot is the winner.

Smile with Kit-Cat®

A SMILE IS SHARING A PART OF YOURSELF WITH OTHERS.

© 1986 CALIFORNIA CLOCK CO.

Kit-Cat™

Smile with Kit-Cat®

A SMILE CAN CHANGE
HOW YOU FEEL ABOUT LIFE!

© 1986 CALIFORNIA CLOCK CO.

ACTIVE PARTY GAMES

★ ★ ★ ★ ★ ★ ★ ★ ★ ★ ★ ★ ★ ★ ★ ★ ★

Holiday Hunt

The old familiar Easter egg hunt can be adapted to any holiday. Simply replace the eggs with another object related to the holiday: Pieces of wrapped holiday candy, or holiday shapes cut from poster board.

Hide the objects outdoors within a designated area, or in one or two rooms inside. At the signal, everyone fans out in an effort to find all the objects possible. The one who finds the most is the winner. You may wish to mark one or more of the objects with a special mark. The guest who finds these will be eligible for prizes. If candy is hidden, each guest is allowed to keep all he finds. If the cardboard shapes are used, let them trade each shape found for a piece of candy, peanut, or other reward.

Holiday Can-Catch

Cover four three-pound coffee cans and decorate for the holiday. Make four holiday-shaped beanbags. Line the cans up, side by side, and mark a line opposite the cans where the players are to stand. Each guest must stand behind the line and attempt to throw one beanbag into each can. Give ten points for each successful attempt. **Note:** *Take into consideration the age and ability of your guests before determining where to mark the line.*

★ ★ ★ ★ ★ ★ ★ ★ ★ ★ ★ ★ ★ ★ ★ ★ ★ ★

★ ★ ★ ★ ★ ★ ★ ★ ★ ★ ★ ★ ★ ★ ★ ★ ★

Drop the Holiday Object

Make a holiday-shaped, felt beanbag and use it in place of a handkerchief for the old "Drop the Handkerchief" game. Have guests stand in a circle, and choose one to be "it." He walks around the outside of the circle with the beanbag in his hand. Without warning, he drops the bag behind someone and starts running around the circle. That person must pick up the bag and run in the opposite direction as fast as he can. The last one to reach the opening is "it" and must drop the bag behind someone else and run as before.

Musical Holiday Candy

Set a table in the middle of the room, or in a place where the group will be able to get around it easily. Put pieces of wrapped holiday candy around the edge of the table, setting out one less than the number of guests. Have the group march around the table to appropriate holiday music. When the music stops, each guest grabs for a piece of candy. The one who is left without a piece must drop out, but he is allowed to eat one piece of the candy. All the other pieces are returned to the table for the next round. Continue until only one person remains to win the prize.

Holiday Trails

Hide appropriate holiday prizes around the room (one for each guest), with a long length of holiday-colored yarn or ribbon attached to each one. Wind each piece of yarn around the furniture, chair and table legs, etc., and attach a holiday-shaped name tag at the end. These name tags can be attached to the wall or be left laying in various places around the room. As guests arrive, have them find their name and roll the yarn around the name tag as they follow the maze to their gift.

★ ★ ★ ★

Holiday Puzzle Run

Cut out a quantity of six-inch holiday shapes from construction paper (about four times as many as the number of guests). Cut each shape in two, using a different zigzag, wavy, or other irregular cut on each one. Put one-half of each shape on a table at one end of the room, and the other half on a table at the other end. Line guests up behind one table. At the signal, each guest picks up half a shape, and goes to the other table to find the matching half. As soon as he finds it, he takes it to a scorekeeper, goes back to the first table for another half, and repeats the action. Set a time limit, and the one who puts together the most shapes during that time is the winner. No guest should be allowed to pick up more than one shape at a time from the first table.

⭐ ⭐ ⭐ ⭐ ⭐ ⭐ ⭐ ⭐ ⭐ ⭐ ⭐

Holiday Party Chairs

Set up two rows of chairs, back to back (one less than the number of guests). Put a self-adhesive holiday seal on each chair back, using two or three different designs. Assign a point value to each different design, i.e., ten points for a star, twenty points for a tree, and thirty points for an angel. (Point values can be changed for each round if you wish.)

Have guests march in a circle around the chairs as you play appropriate holiday music. When the music stops, all guests scramble to get a seat. Announce the point value for each design and have guests report the number of points earned. (The person left without a chair will get no points for that round.) Start the music again, and repeat. Continue for a set length of time or number of rounds. The person with the most accumulated points is the winner.

Variation: Remove one chair at the end of each round, and the person left over must drop out each time. Keep score as above.

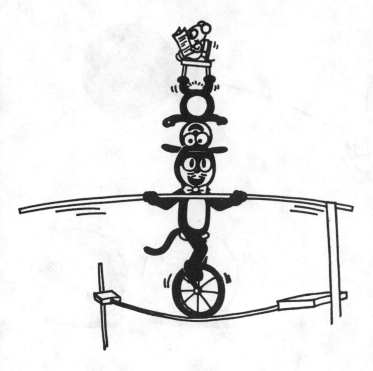

Hot Holiday Symbol

Make a holiday-shaped, felt beanbag or use another holiday symbol, such as a small pumpkin, turkey candle, Christmas tree ornament, heart-shaped box, etc. Seat guests in a circle and start passing the object around as the leader stands with his back to the circle. Every thirty seconds or so, the leader should ring a bell or blow a whistle. Whoever is holding the object when the sound is heard must go to a holiday-decorated box in the center of the circle, and draw out a slip of paper on which is written a stunt he is to perform. After his performance, he goes back to the circle and the game is repeated in the same way as many times as desired. Before you begin, instruct guests that the object may not be thrown, nor can they refuse it when it is offered to them. The person who drops it must pick it up, and it is permissible to reverse directions and send it back the way it came.

Holiday Walk

Cut out twelve-inch holiday shapes, one for each guest. Write a large number on each one with a black felt-tip marker. Tape the shapes in a large circle in the middle of the floor, and have each guest stand on one shape. Instruct guests to walk around the circle, carefully stepping from one shape to the next until the leader calls out: "It's (holiday name)!" Everyone must then stop on one shape and stay there. The leader calls out one number from a prepared list, or draws a number from a decorated box. The person standing on that number receives a treat or small prize. Repeat until all prizes have been given out.

Holiday Balloon Throw

Blow up several balloons in holiday colors, and draw holiday designs all over each one with a felt-tip marker. Mark a line on one side of the room and have guests line up behind it. The object is to see which one can throw their balloon the farthest. Put each contestant's name on a slip of paper and tape it to the floor where his balloon lands.

Holiday Bag Toss

Give each guest a holiday-shaped, felt beanbag. Form a circle and put on a holiday record or other appropriate music. When the music begins, guests start marching around the circle, repeatedly tossing their bag into the air as quickly as possible. Periodically stop the music. Anyone with a beanbag in his hand when the music stops must drop out. Continue until one player remains as a winner.

Holiday Snatch

Make a quantity of holiday shapes cut from poster board or lightweight cardboard (one less than the number of guests). Pile the shapes in the middle of the floor and have guests make a circle around them. Play a holiday song, and when the music stops, everyone rushes to the center to pick up a shape. The person who doesn't get one must drop out. Remove one shape at the end of each round until only one person is left.

Holiday Treasure Hunt

Decorate a lunch-size paper bag for each guest in the holiday motif. Hide a number of small items around the room. In each hiding place put enough of one item for each guest. Hide as many holiday-related items as practical, then use such things as: toothpicks, safety pins, paper clips, marbles, buttons, etc. Make a list of all items and staple a copy to each decorated bag. Give one bag to each guest with instructions that at the signal they are to find each item on their list. When they locate an item, they are to take only one, and not divulge the hiding place. All items are placed in their bag. Give a prize to the first one who finds everything, or to everyone who finds all the things on the list.

Holiday Blind-Toss

You will need about ten holiday-shaped beanbags and a holiday-decorated bucket or box. Line up guests about eight or ten feet from the bucket. (An empty hallway is an ideal place for this game.) As each guest comes to the line, he is given two or three practice throws at the bucket. Blindfold him, and see how many of the bags he can get into the bucket. Keep score for each player. Highest score wins. Play off ties.

Smile with Kit-Cat®

A SMILE IS A POWERFUL TOOL, YOU CAN EVEN BREAK ICE WITH IT!

© 1986 CALIFORNIA CLOCK CO.

WORD GAMES

Holiday Letter Game

Cover two three-pound coffee cans with holiday-colored paper. Cut out a large holiday shape to glue on one side of each can, and use a felt-tip marker to label the shape with its name, i.e., heart, turkey, angel, pumpkin, etc. Place both cans on a table along with a quantity of small slips of paper and a few pencils. Divide the group into two teams and line them up on opposite sides of the room with the table in the center. Assign one can to each team and set it on their side of the table, along with paper and pencils. At the signal, the first person in each line runs to the table and writes any one of the letters in the word written on the can on a slip of paper and throws it into the can. He then runs back to his team and tags the next person in line. Play continues with each team member writing any one of the letters on his slip. At the end of five or ten minutes, blow a whistle or give some other signal. (Each person will have had several turns.) Have each team dump out their can of letters and put the slips together to form the assigned word as many times as possible. The team with the most completed words is the winner.

Words Words

Words

Words **Words**

Holiday Spelling Bee

Have guests form a line across the room, or make a circle around the room, depending on the number of guests and available space. Ahead of time, make up a list of holiday-related words. One at a time, give each guest a word to spell. If he spells the word correctly he remains in line, if not he must sit down and be eliminated. **Note:** *If you do not wish to eliminate players, simply send those who miss words to the end of the line. The best speller will then be the one at the head of the line.*

Words Words

Words

Words

Backwards Holiday Spelling Bee

Play the game the same as "Holiday Spelling Bee," except all words must be spelled backwards. Give a little more time for guests to answer. Since this is a "backwards" game, you may wish to send all those who miss a word to the front of the line.

Words

Words

Words

Words Words

Holiday Chain Words

Make up a list of holiday-related objects, at least one word per guest. Seat guests in a circle, and one at a time assign them one of the words. The object is for that person to tell what that object, and each object in turn makes him think of. For example, if you assign the word "pumpkin," he might say, "Pumpkin makes me think of garden; garden makes me think of dirt; dirt makes me think of worms; worms make me think of fishing; fishing makes me think of water; etc." Give each player one minute. You will need a scorekeeper to keep track of the number of words each person uses, and a timekeeper to call time at the end of a minute. To make it more difficult, you might require that all associations must be related to the holiday.

Holiday Fun Sentences

Divide the group into two or more teams. Give each team a piece of paper and a pencil. Instruct the teams to work together to make up as many sentences as possible in which all the words begin with the same letter as the name of the holiday or a specific holiday object. For example, if the holiday was Christmas, a sentence might be: "Certain cans contain colorful carrots." Set a time limit and then let each team read its sentences. Give a point for each word in every sentence. You might give two points for each holiday-related word used.

Make-A-Holiday-Word

Give each player a pencil and a sheet of paper with a holiday word written across the top. Instruct them to make as many words as they can using only the letters in the word on their paper. Letters can be used in any order; no proper names allowed; and double letters may be used only if there are two of that letter in the original word. Allow five minutes or desired time. Have the one with the most words read his list aloud. Other players may challenge questionable words, and the leader must decide if they are to be allowed. Give a prize to the one with the most approved words.

Holiday Word Jumble

Make up a list of words appropriate to the holiday or occasion. Print the words in large letters on four-inch wide strips of poster board and cut the letters apart (or write letters on individual index cards). Mix up all the letters and lay them upside down on a table between two teams. Have the groups take turns drawing the letters from the table until they are all gone. Give each team a place where they may go to work together to form as many of the holiday words as possible with the letters they have. Give each team a list of the possible words, or write them on a blackboard where they can be seen by both groups. Give ten points for each complete word. Team with the most points wins. **Note:** *If this round goes quickly, you may wish to mix up the cards and play again.*

Holiday Puzzle

Print the name of the holiday, or an appropriate holiday or seasonal word vertically down the center of a sheet of paper. Make up a list of holiday-related words. Each word must contain at least one letter of the word written on the paper. Then make up a list of questions that will correspond with the list of holiday words. Draw in blank spaces for letters on each side of the given letter to show where it falls in the word. Number each letter to correspond with the proper question. Make a copy of the sheet for each guest. Questions may be read orally, or written on the sheet with the puzzle.

For example, a Christmas puzzle might look like this:

```
        1.  C _ _ _ _ _
        2.  _ H _ _ _ _ _ _ _
        3.  _ _ R _
        4.  I _ _
        5.  _ _ S _ _ _ _
        6.  _ _ T _ _ _ _ _ _
        7.  M _ _ _ _
        8.  _ A _ _ _ _
     9.  _ _ _ _ S _
```

1. Christmas song. 2. Heard the angel's message. 3. Mother of Jesus. 4. No room in the _____. 5. Brought gifts to Jesus. 6. Town where Jesus was born. 7. One of the gifts brought to baby Jesus. 8. Bed for baby Jesus. 9. _____child.

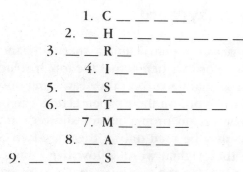

Holiday Macaroni

Pour a large quantity of alphabet macaroni in the middle of a table with the guests seated around it. (Be sure the macaroni can be reached easily by everyone.) Call out a holiday word that must be spelled out with the macaroni letters. Each guest starts searching through the pile of letters and tries to be the first to spell out the assigned word.

Variation: The group may be divided into teams, with each group having its own pile of letters and working together to form the words.

Holiday Word Hunt

Cut paper into two-inch squares. Write out several holiday-related words, one letter to a square. Hide all the squares around the room. Divide group into two teams. At the signal, all team members fan out and find as many of the hidden letters as they can. When all letters have been found, teams reassemble and form as many holiday words as possible with the letters they have found. Give each team a list of possible words. The team to form the most complete words is the winner.

Holiday Lists

Give each guest a sheet of paper and a pencil. At the signal, each one makes a list of objects or words related to the holiday or occasion. For example, a list for Christmas would include: angels, baby Jesus, shepherds, Wise-men, gifts, bells, holly, etc. The one with the longest list at the end of the set time is the winner.

Variation: Divide group into couples or teams and let them work together on a list.

Holiday Word Finder

Make up a list of fifteen to eighteen holiday-related words. Use those words to make a word-finder puzzle, hiding the holiday words vertically, horizontally, and diagonally among unrelated letters in even rows. Duplicate the puzzle for each guest, with a list of included words. Give a set length of time to complete the puzzle. The first one to finish, or to find the most words within the set time is the winner.

Holiday Word Relay

Divide the group into two relay teams. Set up two chalkboards at the goal line, or hang two large sheets of paper on the wall at the end of the room. Print the name of the holiday, or a holiday object, in large letters across the top of each board or paper. Line up teams at the opposite end of the room. The object is for team members to take turns running to the board and writing a word. The catch is that each word written must use only the letters in the word at the top, and no word may be used more than once. The team to finish first, with all words correct, is the winner. If your teams are small, you may set a time limit rather than giving each person only one turn. In that case, the team that comes up with the most words within the time limit will be the winner.

Holiday Team Bee

Make up a list of holiday-related words. Divide the group into two or more teams, and assign a word to one team at a time. The catch is that each person may give only one letter of the assigned word. The first one in line gives the first letter, the second person the next letter, and so on until the word is completed. If anyone fails to give the next correct consecutive letter, the team loses its point for that word. Give one point for each correctly spelled word. When one team has completed a word, go on to the next team in the same way. When you come back to the first team with a new word, start where you left off in the line, don't begin with the first person again. Set a time limit for the whole game, and keep score for each team, being sure each team is given the opportunity to spell an equal number of words.

Holiday Word Bag

Make up a list of holiday-related words. Write the letters needed to spell out those words on one-inch squares of paper. Make two or more identical sets of letters and put each set in a lunch-size bag decorated appropriately for the holiday. Divide the group into two or more teams; seat teams in individual circles, and give them each a sack of letters. The leader calls out one word from the list which the teams must spell out with their letters. The sack is passed around the circle, and each team member draws out one letter. If it is needed to spell the given word, it is set aside. If not, it is returned to the bag before the bag is passed on to the next person. The first team to complete the assigned word is the winner of that round and earns five points. Repeat as many times as you like, using different words from the list. The team with the highest score at the end is the winner.

★ ★ ★ ★ ★ ★ ★

★ ★ ★ ★ ★ ★ ★

Crazy Holiday Objects

Make up a list of holiday-related objects and divide the group into two teams. Give each team several sheets of paper and a pencil. Ask both teams at once, "What can you do with a (*Christmas tree*)? (Fill the blank with an object from your list.) Each team then works together to make a list of all the crazy things they might do with the named object. After a set time, let each team read its list, and then decide which group came up with the most original uses. Repeat the question several times with a different object.

MEMORY GAMES

☆ ☆ ☆ ☆ ☆ ☆ ☆   ☆ ☆ ☆ ☆ ☆ ☆ ☆

Holiday Fishing

Cut out a quantity of four-inch holiday shapes from construction paper. Write a Bible reference or a question on each shape, and attach a paper clip at the top. Drop the shapes into a decorated bowl, basket, or wastepaper basket. Make a fishing pole from a dowel or a stick with a string and magnet attached. Let each guest "fish" for a shape. If he can recite the verse or answer the question correctly, he is allowed to hold the shape. If he is incorrect, it goes back into the container. To add interest, you may want to add a star to three of the shapes which will be redeemable for a holiday treat if answered correctly.

Holiday Lollipop Review

Purchase a quantity of holiday lollipops or plain, cellophane-wrapped lollipops and add a holiday seal to each wrapper. Have enough for at least one per guest. Put a colored dot on the ends of two or three of the lollipop sticks. Poke all the sticks into a Styrofoam cone or slab, or into a decorated cardboard box deep enough to hide the ends of the sticks and allow the lollipops to stand upright. Hand each guest the start of a verse written on a holiday symbol. Each guest who can recites his memory verse (or other assigned verse) correctly, is allowed to choose a lollipop. Those who select the ones with the colored tips are given a special reward, or an extra lollipop to take home.

Variation: Let guests pick a lollipop when they have answered a question correctly.

Sweet Holiday Questions

Cut a large holiday shape from a sheet of poster board and tack it to a bulletin board. Use straight pins to cover the shape with pieces of wrapped candy or stick straight pins all over the shape and hang a Lifesaver on each pin. Ask each guest a question. If he answers correctly, he may take a piece of candy from the shape.

Holiday Egg Review

Decorate a dozen L'eggs eggs to fit the holiday. Put a question in each egg, along with a piece of holiday candy. Each guest in turn chooses an egg. If he can answer the enclosed question correctly, he gets to eat the treat. **Note:** *You can make stands for the eggs by decorating 1 x 6 inch strips of construction paper and stapling the ends together to make a ring, or pile the eggs in an appropriately decorated box or basket.*

Competition Bee

Competition bees have been around for a long time. Many examples can be used: spelling bee, math bee, capitol bee, movie information, company information (policies, safety, etc.). The following is an example of how to do a Capitol Bee. Form circles consisting of ten to fifteen guests. Ask participants to stand up. Go around the group, asking state capitol questions at random. As a participant misses, ask him/her to sit down. The last person standing wins a prize.

State	Capitol	State	Capitol
Alabama	- Montgomery	Montana	- Helena
Alaska	- Juneau	Nebraska	- Lincoln
Arizona	- Phoenix	Nevada	- Carson City
Arkansas	- Little Rock	New Hampshire	- Concord
California	- Sacramento	New Jersey	- Trenton
Colorado	- Denver	New Mexico	- Santa Fe
Connecticut	- Hartford	New York	- Albany
Delaware	- Dover	North Carolina	- Raleigh
Florida	- Tallahassee	North Dakota	- Bismarck
Georgia	- Atlanta	Ohio	- Columbus
Hawaii	- Honolulu	Oklahoma	- Oklahoma City
Idaho	- Boise	Oregon	- Salem
Illinois	- Springfield	Pennsylvania	- Harrisburg
Indiana	- Indianapolis	Rhode Island	- Providence
Iowa	- Des Moines	South Carolina	- Columbia
Kansas	- Topeka	South Dakota	- Pierre
Kentucky	- Frankfort	Tennessee	- Nashville
Louisiana	- Baton Rouge	Texas	- Austin
Maine	- Augusta	Utah	- Salt Lake
Maryland	- Annapolis	Vermont	- Montpelier
Massachusetts	- Boston	Virginia	- Richmond
Michigan	- Lansing	Washington	- Olympia
Minnesota	- St. Paul	West Virginia	- Charleston
Mississippi	- Jackson	Wisconsin	- Madison
Missouri	- Jefferson City	Wyoming	- Cheyenne

Holiday Pop

Collect a number of balloons in appropriate holiday colors. On individual slips of paper, write numbered questions. Fold each question and put it inside a balloon. Inflate the balloons and tie. Draw holiday designs on each balloon with a felt-tip pen. One at a time, have each guest select a balloon, pop it, and answer the enclosed question. If he is correct, he wins a corresponding numbered prize or holiday treat.

Holiday Question Hunt

Cut small holiday shapes from construction paper, number them consecutively, and hide them around the room. Make up a list of questions and number them to correspond with the hidden numbers. Have guests find all the hidden shapes, hold the ones they find, and then take their seats. Call out the numbers consecutively and ask the question (from your sheet) of the guest holding that number. If he answers the question correctly, he keeps the shape. If not, it goes to the first one who can answer it. A holiday-related prize may go to the guest holding the most shapes at the end.

Variation: Each shape can be assigned a point value, according to the difficulty of the question, as well as a number. Then the person earning the most points for correctly answered questions will be the winner.

Holiday Pin-Up

Cut a large holiday shape from a sheet of poster board, and tack it to a bulletin board. Write out questions on small sheets of paper (a 3 x 5 scratch pad works well), and fold into fourths. Add a holiday seal to the front of each folded sheet and pin to the holiday shape with straight pins. Cover the shape evenly with questions. Guests take turns selecting a question and trying to answer it. If their answer is correct, they may keep it. If not, it is pinned back on the board for another to answer. Give a prize to the one who answers the most questions correctly.

Holiday Shape Mixer

Cut out a quantity of four-inch holiday shapes in pairs from construction paper. Fill in the pairs of shapes in one of the ways described in "Holiday Match Game." Give out the shapes, one to a guest, and have each one find the person with the matching shape. When all the shapes have been matched, they can be collected, shuffled, and redistributed for another round.

Holiday Tic-Tac-Toe

Cut four long narrow strips of black felt and overlap to make a tic-tac-toe grid on a flannelboard. Also cut five each of two different holiday shapes (or the same shape in two different colors) out of felt. Divide your group into two teams, select a captain for each, and give each captain the five shapes for his team. Prepare a list of questions ahead of time. The captains take turns choosing someone from their team to answer a question, being sure everyone gets a turn. If the question is answered correctly, the captain is allowed to put up one of the shapes, playing the same as a regular game of tic-tac-toe. If an answer is incorrect, the team cannot put up a shape, and the next question goes to the opposing team. The first team to put three shapes in a row is the winner of that round. Continue playing as long as you have questions to ask. Questions that are missed can be repeated later in the game.

Holiday Jigsaw Puzzle

Find or draw two large, holiday pictures or figures and cut them into an equal number of irregular pieces to make puzzles. Divide the group into two teams and give each team the pieces of one puzzle. Alternately ask questions of each team. If the team is able to answer their question, they may add one piece to their puzzle. If they do not answer correctly, no piece is added, and the question is asked of the other team. The first team to complete their puzzle is the winner. **Note:** *For younger players you may need to outline the position of each puzzle on a sheet of paper to help them assemble it more easily.*

Holiday Match Game

Cut out twenty-four four-inch holiday shapes from construction paper. This game can be adapted to several different types of information. Select the adaptation that best suits your current needs: (1) Write the name of a Bible character on one shape, and a related character on another (David-Goliath), using twelve different pairs to fill all twenty-four shapes; (2) Write the name of a Bible character on one and a related object on the other (Noah-ark); (3) Write a brief question on one, and the answer on another; (4) Write the first half of a memory verse on one, and the remaining half on the other.

Lay the prepared shapes face down on the floor (or a table), and have guests sit in a circle around them. Shapes must be arranged in four even rows of six. Players take turns turning over one shape, and then a second, trying to make a match. If a player is successful in making a match, he keeps the two shapes and is allowed another turn. (He does not lose his turn until he fails to make a match.) If a match is not made, the shapes must be returned to their original positions, and the next player takes a turn. Continue playing until all matches have been made. The one who holds the most shapes at the end is the winner.

Holiday Concentration

Prepare a game board on a 22 x 28 inch sheet of poster board in the holiday color. Glue on sixteen library pockets in four even rows of four. (In place of library pockets, you may seal eight legal-size envelopes and cut each in half to make two pockets.) Decorate the front of each pocket with a holiday seal and number them consecutively from 1-16. You will also need sixteen 3 x 5 inch index cards, and eight different pairs of holiday seals. Put one seal on the back of each card (or draw two each of eight different holiday shapes). The two cards with the matching seal or shape will form a pair and should be prepared for this game by filling in the appropriate information, using one of the methods described in "Holiday Match Game" (page 70). When all cards have been prepared in like manner, they are mixed up and placed one in a pocket. The question should be facing the front (although hidden within the pocket) and the seal will be facing the back. The idea again is to find the two matching cards. The leader pulls out two cards at random to get the game started. Each guest takes a turn calling out the number of the two pockets he thinks will match. The leader displays the two cards chosen, and the group must decide whether or not a match has been made. When they have made their decision, verify it by turning the two cards over. If the designs on the back are the same, it is a match. If a match is made, that guest gets to hold the cards. If not, the cards are returned to their envelopes, and the next guest makes a guess. Continue until all matches are made.

Smile   with Kit-Cat®

A SMILE IS THE SAME IN ALL LANGUAGES!

© 1986 CALIFORNIA CLOCK CO.

Kit Cat™

BRAIN TEASERS (8)

PUZZLE

Inch Worm

If an inch worm eats through a set of books, starting at the first page of the first book, and eating through the last page of the last book; and there are ten books, each being 2 inches thick; how many inches will he eat if all of the books are standing together in numerical order? The answer is 16.

How Many Squares?

This exercise points out the importance of using a systematic approach to working through a complex task. Divide the group into teams of two. Ask them to count the number of squares in the HOW MANY SQUARES HANDOUT. The team closest to the correct number wins. There are at least 63.

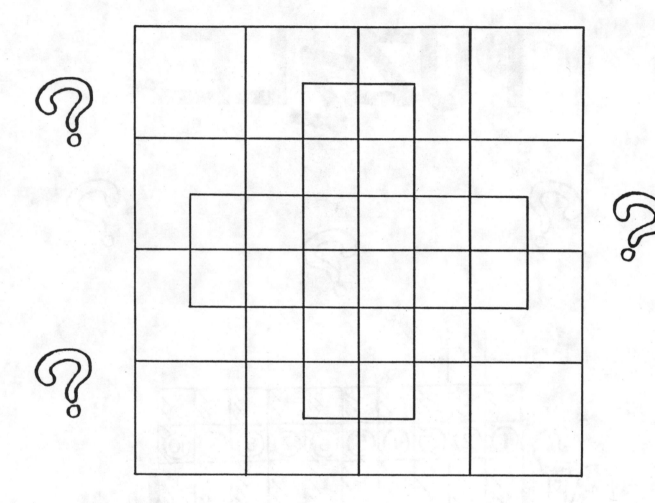

PUZZLE

What is the only number spelled with the exact number of letters it stands for? Answer: 4.

Multiply what number by any whole number other than zero and the resulting digits will always add up to nine? The answer is 9.

How can you rearrange the letters: EDORNOW into one word? Answer: ONE WORD.

Can you make sense out of these word configurations? Each is a complete thought as presented.

STAND TAKE   TO TAKING

  I   YOU THROW MY

I understand you undertake to overthrow my undertaking.

That that is is that that is not is not is not that it it is

The above can be made to make sense by adding:
1 semicolon
1 question mark
2 commas
2 periods

That that is, is; that that is not, is not. Is not that it? It is.

Pronounced as one letter, and written with three, two letters there are, and two only in me. I'm double, I'm single, I'm black, blue and gray. I'm read from both ends, and the same either way.

The word: "eye".

STOOL HE FELL STOOL

He fell between two stools.

I lose my head when I'm here. Transpose me I am three. Look in a book, you find me there. And with me, her and he.

The word: "there".

Smile with Kit-Cat®

A SMILE BRINGS OUT THE BEST IN YOU!

© 1986 CALIFORNIA CLOCK CO.

HELPFUL HINTS TO BETTER PLANNED PARTIES

Hosting a party is like building a powerful rocket—once the rocket is built, a flight plan needs to be developed. In order to make your party "fly", you need to take several preparatory actions:

ACTION ONE: Develop a "script" which will include what you are going to say and the instructions for each activity.

ACTION TWO: Make a list of the materials, equipment, handouts, and prizes needed for each activity.

ACTION THREE: Determine the room arrangement including the placement of the tables and chairs. This assures adequate space for subgroups.

Keep the Party Moving
For a livelier party it's always best to have more guests than seating. This will keep your guests mingling, rather than sitting down!

A House Warming
Save energy and keep everyone comfortable by lowering the thermostat before guests arrive. A roomful of people heats up quickly.

Energy Saving (Yours!)
Just a reminder: arrange all the foods you'll need on one shelf in the refrigerator. It's easier to remove—and you won't forget to serve any of it!

APPETIZERS

Out of the Freezer, Onto the Hors d'oeuvres Tray

Defrost cheese-or meat-filled tortellini and cook them according to the directions on the package. Toss them with a light garlic dressing, sprinkle with Parmesan and serve with toothpicks.

Defrost a box of spinach souffle', then spoon into large, fresh mushroom caps until filled but not overflowing. Bake in a 375 oven for about fifteen minutes. Recipe yields about two dozen.

REFRESHMENTS

Prettier Ice Cubes
Drop a rose petal into each compartment of an ice-cube tray. Fill with water, then freeze. This looks terrific floating in a drink.
Or, try lemon peel.
Or, strawberries.
Or, mint leaves.
Or, candied violets.

Extra Ice Cube Trays
Use Styrofoam egg cartons as trays when you need extra ice for parties.

Out of Ginger Ale?
Mix equal parts of Coke and 7-Up. You won't be able to tell the difference.

CAKES

Icing Ideas for Birthdays or Valentine's Day

Add a small amount of red, unsweetened powdered drink mix to powdered sugar frosting. You'll get a pink color and great flavor.

If you use lots of maraschino cherries, save the juice and substitute for some of the liquid in your cake batter mix. Cherry juice turns the cake mix pink and adds a touch of sweetening.

This Hint's Write-on!
When decorating on cake frosting, trace the design or message with a toothpick. Then use an empty mustard squeeze bottle filled with frosting to fill it in.

GUEST LIST

	NAME	ADDRESS	CITY	STATE	PHONE	NO. INVITED
1.						
2.						
3.						
4.						
5.						
6.						
7.						
8.						
9.						
10.						
11.						
12.						
13.						
14.						
15.						
16.						
17.						
18.						
19.						
20.						
21.						
22.						
23.						
24.						
25.						

BE IT KNOWN THAT

IS PRESENTED WITH THIS AWARD FOR A

JOB WELL DONE

DATE

SIGNATURE

THIS AWARD IS PRESENTED TO

FOR

WILLINGNESS TO TRY

SIGNATURE

DATE

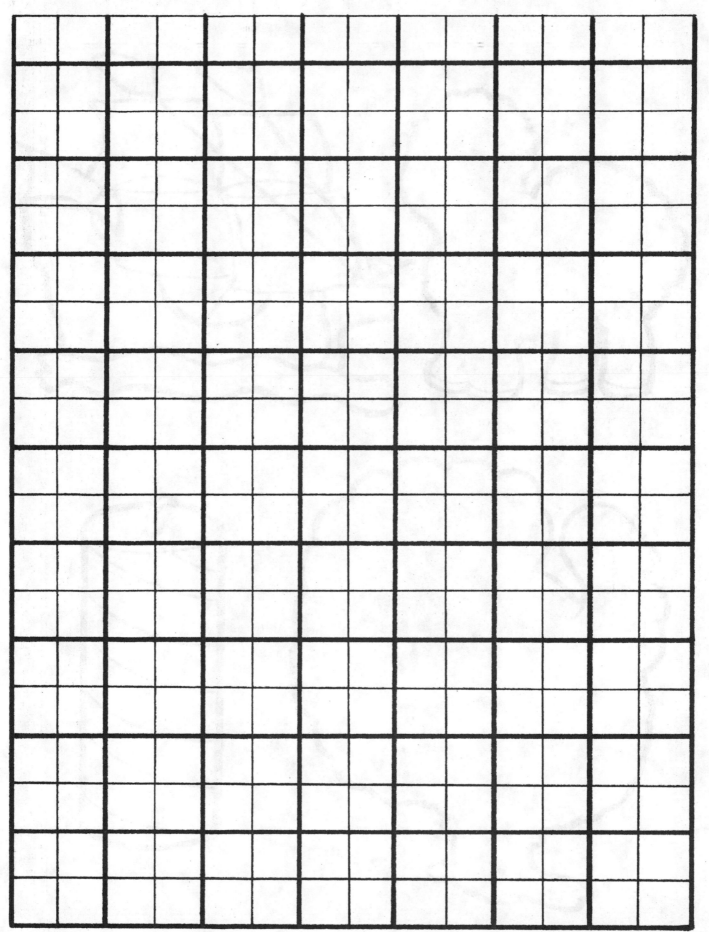

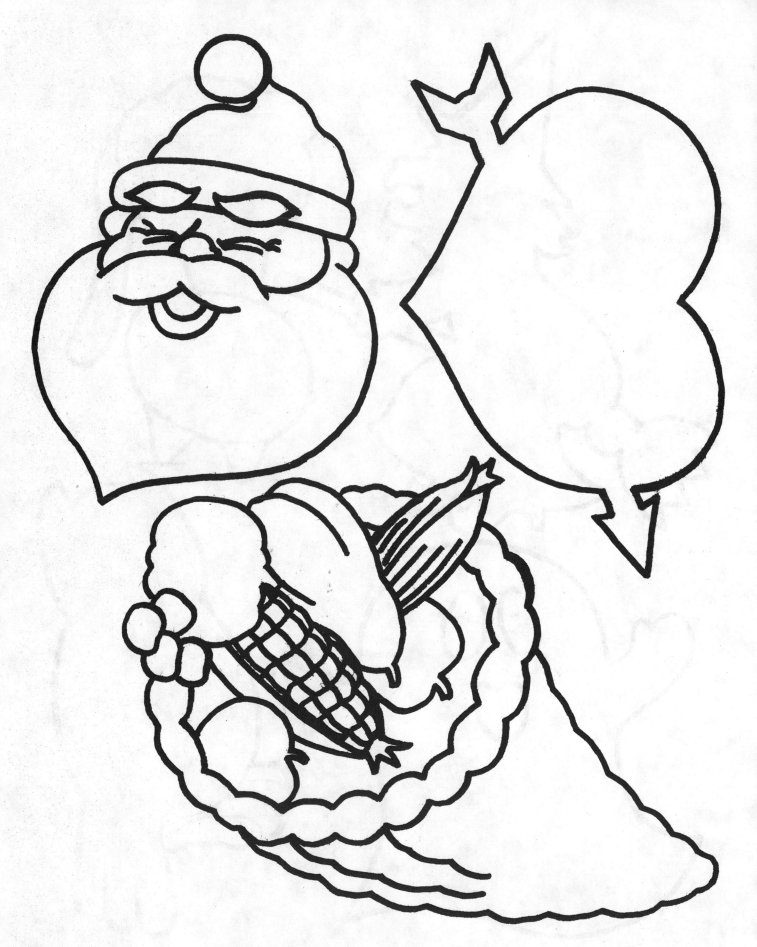

Smile with Kit-Cat®

KIT-CAT® LIBRARY

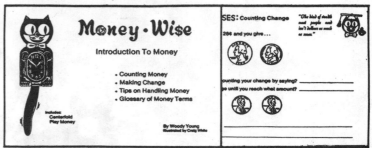

Smile Wise

Designed to be a source of inspiration for all ages, Smilewise is a collection of "Smile with Kit-Cat®" cartoons. Each cartoon illustrates how we can make this world a better place as easily as with a smile. 48 pages. **SMW**

4.95 ea.

Moneywise

Designed for children ages 6-10, Moneywise takes a brief look at the history of money and its uses and then teaches children how to count pennies, nickels, dimes, quarters and dollar bills. Exercises, giving practice in addition and subtraction and in making change using play money cut-outs, makes for hours of fun and education! **MW**   4.95 ea.

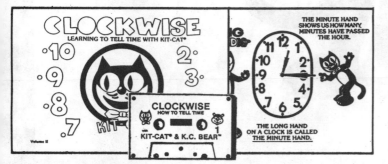

Clockwise Learn to Tell Time

Written for children ages 4-10, Kit-Cat® teaches them how to tell time. A paper model Kit-Cat Klock® is included for practice, as well as games, puzzles and exercises. 48 pages. **CW**   4.95 ea.

Cassette Tape   with tape 14.95 set.

"How to Tell Time with Kit-Cat® and KC Bear™". Cassette is a 50 minute, 6 part lesson which follows the "Clockwise Learn to Tell Time" book. The characters of Kit-Cat® and KC Bear™ bring the book to life as they entertain while they teach. **CWT**

Babysitting Wise

Babysitting Wise is an exceptional tool for parents and babysitters. Recently, it has received acclaim through newspaper reviews and radio station broadcasts across the nation. Once completed by parents, babysitters have a handy reference for doctor and emergency phone numbers, fire escape procedures, helpful hints for handling children and much more! A Kit-Cat® saying and illustration is also featured on each page. This is a book that no household with children should be without! 48 pages. **BW**

4.95 ea.

Clockwise Quotes on Life

Kit-Cat® has learned some important aspects about life through the years. Now, he's sharing his positive thoughts with you in this delightful book written for all ages to enjoy. Each page comes to life with a motivational saying and uplifting illustration that you will treasure for years to come! 48 pages **CWQ**   4.95 ea.

Song Wise Books

This delightful series of books brings the words of our country's most patriotic songs to life. Each book begins with the history of the song and then continues by illustrating each verse for easy recall and includes its melody note line. Kit-Cat's® hope is that this will bring meaning to the words, making them more enjoyable to sing and rekindling a great admiration for our country and what she stands for. Books for all ages to share and enjoy!

SOW-1 Star Spangled Banner	2.95 ea.
SOW-2 America the Beautiful	2.95 ea.
SOW-3 Battle Hymn of the Republic	2.95 ea.
SOW-4 America	2.95 ea.

Each book is 24 pages.   **95**

KIT-CAT® CREED

PUT A SMILE ON EVERYONES FACE
LOVE IN EVERYONES HEART
AND ENERGY IN EVERYONES BODY
BE A POSITIVE FORCE IN EVERYONES LIFE

For information about how you can join the Kit-Cat® Fan Club
Write To: KIT-CAT® FAN CLUB
   % California Clock Co.
   Box 827- G1
   San Juan Capistrano, CA 92675

Other Kit-Cat® products available for your enjoyment:
   T-Shirts, Stickers, Mugs, Posters, Buttons, Magnets, Rulers,
   Bookmarks, Pencils, Note Pads, Mug Rugs, Planters, Aprons,
   Books, Pins and Greeting Cards.